WO?

VALENTINE'S
EDITION : VOLUME 2

TRY NOT TO LAUGH® CHALLENGE

TM & Copyright© 2020 by Try Not To Laugh Challenge Group®

ALL RIGHTS RESERVED.

Published in the United States. By purchase of this book, you have been licensed one copy for personal use only. No part of this work may be reproduced, redistributed, or used in any form or by any means without prior written permission of the publisher and copyright owner.

Try Not To Laugh Challenge®
BONUS PLAY

Join our Joke Club and get the Bonus Play PDF!

Simply send us an email to:

 TNTLPublishing@gmail.com

and you will get the following:

- 10 Hilarious Would You Rather Questions
- An entry in our Monthly Giveaway of a $50 Amazon Gift card!

We draw a new winner each month and will contact you via email!
Good luck!

Welcome to
The Try Not to Laugh Challenge®
Would You Rather?
♥ VALENTINE'S EDITION ♥
VOL. 2

RULES:

- Face your opponent and decide who is Player 1 and Player 2.

- Starting with Player 1, read the Would You Rather question aloud and pick an answer. The same player will then explain why they chose that answer in the most hilarious or wacky way possible!

- If the reason makes Player 2 laugh, then a laugh point is scored!

- Take turns going back and forth, then mark your total laugh points at the end of each round!

- Whoever gets the most laugh points is officially crowned The Laugh Master!

- If ending with a tie, finish with the Tie-Breaker round for WINNER TAKES ALL!

Most importantly, have fun and be SILLY!

REMEMBER, these scenarios listed in the book are solely for fun and games! Please do <u>NOT</u> attempt any of the crazy scenarios in this book.

Player

(DON'T FORGET TO EXPLAIN YOUR ANSWERS!)

Would you rather hold hands with someone whose palms were super sweaty, OR hold hands with someone whose fingers were covered in nacho cheese?

Laugh Point____/1

Would you rather have rose petals fly out of your nose, every time you sneezed OR shoot jelly beans out of your mouth, every time you coughed?

Laugh Point____/1

Player 1

(DON'T FORGET TO EXPLAIN YOUR ANSWERS!)

Would you rather have to crawl through a mile-long tunnel filled with melted gummy bears, OR bungee jump from the top of a bridge using an extra-stretchy band of licorice?

Laugh Point____/1

Would you rather replace all Valentine's Day candy with canned vegetables, OR get a papercut every time you open a Valentine's card?

Laugh Point____/1

Pass the book to Player 2 →

Player 2

(DON'T FORGET TO EXPLAIN YOUR ANSWERS!)

Would you rather have your hair be made of Pixie Stix OR have all of your fingers become heart-shaped lollipops?

Laugh Point____/1

Would you rather have Cupid's wings, so you could fly anywhere OR have Cupid's arrow, so you could make anyone fall in love?

Laugh Point____/1

Player 2

(DON'T FORGET TO EXPLAIN YOUR ANSWERS!)

Would you rather celebrate every Valentine's Day by jumping into a pool of chocolate-covered strawberries OR by taking a hot chocolate shower?

Laugh Point____/1

Would you rather have eyeballs in the shape of hearts OR have ears in the shape of arrows?

Laugh Point____/1

Time to score your points! →

Add up your scores and record them below!

Player  ___ /4
ROUND TOTAL

Player  ___ /4
ROUND TOTAL

ROUND CHAMPION

Player 1

(DON'T FORGET TO EXPLAIN YOUR ANSWERS!)

Would you rather have to eat 800 lbs. of your least favorite candy, OR have to fight an 800-pound gorilla to keep all of your candy?

Laugh Point____/1

Would you rather have the word LOVE written in permanent marker across your forehead all day on Valentine's, OR have your entire body covered in red and pink glitter?

Laugh Point____/1

Player 1

(DON'T FORGET TO EXPLAIN YOUR ANSWERS!)

Would you rather accidentally give every one of your classmates a Valentine's card that said, "I LOVE YOU, XOXO" OR give out every Valentine's card in an envelope filled with your own toenail clippings?

Laugh Point____/1

Would you rather have Frankenstein fall madly in love with you, OR have a hoard of zombies follow you everywhere you went?

Laugh Point____/1

Pass the book to Player 2 →

Player

(DON'T FORGET TO EXPLAIN YOUR ANSWERS!)

Would you rather have a time machine that could go back in time to erase any embarrassing moments, OR have an earpiece from the future that allowed you to read minds?

Laugh Point____/1

Would you rather have angel wings, but have to wear a diaper OR have no wings, but get to wear your normal underwear?

Laugh Point____/1

Player 2

(DON'T FORGET TO EXPLAIN YOUR ANSWERS!)

Would you rather receive a beautiful bouquet of flowers that made you sneeze all day and night, OR receive a talking teddy bear that randomly yelled out insults throughout the day?

Laugh Point____/1

Would you rather be able to choose what you dream about every night, OR choose who you fall in love with in the future?

Laugh Point____/1

Time to score your points! →

Add up your scores and record them below!

Player  1 ___/4
ROUND TOTAL

Player 2 ___/4
ROUND TOTAL

ROUND CHAMPION

Player 1

(DON'T FORGET TO EXPLAIN YOUR ANSWERS!)

Would you rather have your mom pick up your crush and surprise you, OR for your crush to bring his mom to your study date?

Laugh Point____/1

Would you rather suddenly grow a unibrow whenever you walked up to someone you thought was cute, OR go bald during the first 10 seconds someone cute walked up to you?

Laugh Point____/1

Player 1

(DON'T FORGET TO EXPLAIN YOUR ANSWERS!)

Would you rather kiss a bullfrog that gave you warts, but also gave you 3 wishes OR marry an ogre that gave you lice, but also a million dollars?

Laugh Point____/1

Would you rather meet a mad scientist who made all your Valentine's candy come to life, OR meet a magician who made all of your Valentine's candy disappear, then reappear?

Laugh Point____/1

Pass the book to Player 2 →

Player

(DON'T FORGET TO EXPLAIN YOUR ANSWERS!)

Would you rather spend your Valentine's Day embraced by a giant, slimy squid all day OR spend it with a Yeti holding you upside down by your shoe?

Laugh Point____/1

Would you rather never taste sugar again OR never eat your favorite food again?

Laugh Point____/1

Player 2

(DON'T FORGET TO EXPLAIN YOUR ANSWERS!)

Would you rather cry tears made of the juice in Fruit Gushers, OR every time you clipped your nails, the nail clippings turned into candy?

Laugh Point____/1

Would you rather only be able to talk by rhyming every sentence, OR only be able to speak if you whispered everything you said?

Laugh Point____/1

Time to score your points! →

Add up your scores and record them below!

Player  **1**   _____ /4
ROUND TOTAL

Player **2**   _____ /4
ROUND TOTAL

_____
ROUND CHAMPION

Player

(DON'T FORGET TO EXPLAIN YOUR ANSWERS!)

Would you rather have every Valentine's card be replaced with a giant dill pickle, OR have to eat one giant dill pickle for every 5 pieces of candy you ate?

Laugh Point____/1

Would you rather laugh uncontrollably every time you ate a piece of cake, OR have a kitten appear every time you ate a chocolate bar?

Laugh Point____/1

Player 1

(DON'T FORGET TO EXPLAIN YOUR ANSWERS!)

Would you rather only be able to eat dessert that doesn't contain chocolate OR only eat chocolate, but never be able to eat other desserts?

Laugh Point____/1

Would you rather kiss someone who told the entire school you both kissed, OR kiss someone who never stopped talking during your kiss?

Laugh Point____/1

Pass the book to Player 2 →

Player

(DON'T FORGET TO EXPLAIN YOUR ANSWERS!)

Would you rather kayak down a milkshake waterfall OR live in a treehouse made out of Tootsie Pops?

Laugh Point____/1

Would you rather have a loud siren go off every time you saw someone you thought was cute, OR hear a bunch of monkeys start howling whenever you talked to your crush?

Laugh Point____/1

Player

(DON'T FORGET TO EXPLAIN YOUR ANSWERS!)

Would you rather sweat liquid chocolate OR have every hair on your body grow an inch, every hour?

Laugh Point____/1

Would you rather enter every room by floating on a seashell like Aphrodite, the Goddess of Love OR go to sleep every night in a giant, heart-shaped box of chocolates?

Laugh Point____/1

Time to score your points! →

Add up your scores and record them below!

Player  /4
ROUND TOTAL

Player ❤2 /4
ROUND TOTAL

_____
ROUND CHAMPION

Player ♥1

(DON'T FORGET TO EXPLAIN YOUR ANSWERS!)

Would you rather take a shower in pink water OR brush your teeth with purple toothpaste that turned your tongue blue?

Laugh Point____/1

Would you rather realize you went to school only half dressed, OR get locked in at school overnight by mistake?

Laugh Point____/1

Player 1

(DON'T FORGET TO EXPLAIN YOUR ANSWERS!)

Would you rather get trapped in a maze made of melting ice cream OR have to climb a mountain that's made of frozen popsicles?

Laugh Point____/1

Would you rather encounter a stampede of angry flamingos running through your school on Valentine's Day, OR have one calm, cool, and collected T-Rex strolling through your school's hallways?

Laugh Point____/1

Pass the book to Player 2 →

Player

(DON'T FORGET TO EXPLAIN YOUR ANSWERS!)

Would you rather be in charge of Cupid's bow and arrow and have the ability to make anyone fall in love, OR be in charge of Willy Wonka's Chocolate Factory making enough candy for Valentine's Day?

Laugh Point____/1

Would you rather have to spin 10x before you talked to your crush OR have to walk everywhere on your hands?

Laugh Point____/1

Player 2

(DON'T FORGET TO EXPLAIN YOUR ANSWERS!)

Would you rather replace all spoons and forks with Fun Dip candy sticks, OR have every food be in powder-form like Fun Dip?

Laugh Point____/1

Would you rather have to slow dance with someone you don't get along with OR have to hug a complete stranger?

Laugh Point____/1

Time to score your points! →

Add up your scores and record them below!

Player  1 ___ /4
ROUND TOTAL

Player 2 ___ /4
ROUND TOTAL

___ ROUND CHAMPION

Player ❤ 1

(DON'T FORGET TO EXPLAIN YOUR ANSWERS!)

Would you rather jump on a trampoline made out of stretched out Bazooka bubblegum, OR float down from the sky using a parachute made of marshmallows?

Laugh Point____/1

Would you rather have to blow a kiss to 10 strangers every Valentine's Day OR give a stranger a 10-second hug?

Laugh Point____/1

Player

(DON'T FORGET TO EXPLAIN YOUR ANSWERS!)

Would you rather have to build a 5-story pyramid using only chocolate bars, OR have to eat 5 gallons of chocolate pudding in one sitting?

Laugh Point____/1

Would you rather tell the wrong person you love them on Valentine's Day, OR have every single person you know confess their love for you?

Laugh Point____/1

Player

(DON'T FORGET TO EXPLAIN YOUR ANSWERS!)

Would you rather have a tornado pick your entire school building in the air and place you on a desert island, OR spend your Valentine's Day getting stuck in a video game where you're being hunted?

Laugh Point____/1

Would you rather have your tongue be made out of bubblegum OR your eyebrows be made out of cotton candy?

Laugh Point____/1

Player 2

(DON'T FORGET TO EXPLAIN YOUR ANSWERS!)

Would you rather have to walk up to your crush on Valentine's Day and sing them a love song, OR slow dance by yourself to a love song in front of all your classmates?

Laugh Point____/1

Would you rather faint every time your crush came up to you, and by the time you woke up they were gone OR sneeze right in your crush's face whenever they glanced at you?

Laugh Point____/1

Time to score your points! →

Add up your scores and record them below!

Player  1 ____ /4
ROUND TOTAL

Player ♥ 2 ____ /4
ROUND TOTAL

____ ROUND CHAMPION

ROUND 7

Player 1

(DON'T FORGET TO EXPLAIN YOUR ANSWERS!)

Would you rather be haunted by the ghosts of everyone you ever had a crush on, OR be constantly followed by everyone who ever had a crush on you?

Laugh Point____/1

Would you rather have every love song have your name in it, OR have someone sing a love song to you once every day?

Laugh Point____/1

Player 1

(DON'T FORGET TO EXPLAIN YOUR ANSWERS!)

Would you rather spend Valentine's Day abducted by aliens who made you eat their weird space candy, OR spend it captured by pirates who took all of your candy to bury beneath the sea?

Laugh Point____/1

Would you rather hold the title of King/Queen of Candy Mountain, OR be the Prince/Princess of Popsicles and Pastries?

Laugh Point____/1

Pass the book to Player 2 →

Player 2

(DON'T FORGET TO EXPLAIN YOUR ANSWERS!)

Would you rather have one of your teeth fall out in the middle of kissing someone OR be given a locket necklace as a Valentine's Day gift, only to find a tooth inside?

Laugh Point____/1

Would you rather be forced to read your teacher's love letters OR read every text your mom ever sent?

Laugh Point____/1

Player

(DON'T FORGET TO EXPLAIN YOUR ANSWERS!)

Would you rather listen to love stories told by a mysterious cat, OR listen to random stories from the world's most ancient tree?

Laugh Point____/1

Would you rather have to pick up 1,000 Nerd candies using only tweezers, OR have to hold 20 sour Warhead candies in your mouth until they dissolved?

Laugh Point____/1

Time to score your points! →

Add up your scores and record them below!

Player  **1**   /4
          ─────────
         ROUND TOTAL

Player 2   /4
         ─────────
         ROUND TOTAL

_____
ROUND CHAMPION

Player

(DON'T FORGET TO EXPLAIN YOUR ANSWERS!)

Would you rather have a belly button on each hand OR a miniature hand sticking out of your belly button?

Laugh Point____/1

Would you rather have Santa Claus leave you a present on Valentine's Day, OR have the Tooth Fairy leave money under your pillow on Valentine's Day?

Laugh Point____/1

Player 1

(DON'T FORGET TO EXPLAIN YOUR ANSWERS!)

Would you rather kiss someone whose lips were chapped and crusty OR kiss someone who slobbered all over you?

Laugh Point____/1

Would you rather have a fortune teller look into their crystal ball and show you who you will marry, OR have a palm reader tell you the name of everyone who has a crush on you?

Laugh Point____/1

Pass the book to Player 2 →

Player

(DON'T FORGET TO EXPLAIN YOUR ANSWERS!)

Would you rather have a wad of bubblegum permanently stuck in your hair, OR have to wear a Ring Pop on every other finger at all times?

Laugh Point_____/1

Would you rather go cave diving to search for precious, rare candies OR receive an unlimited supply of one candy of your choice, but that was the only candy you could ever eat?

Laugh Point_____/1

Player 2

(DON'T FORGET TO EXPLAIN YOUR ANSWERS!)

Would you rather grow an extra foot every time you ate a Fruit by the Foot, OR grow an extra mouth every time you ate a Hershey's Kiss?

Laugh Point____/1

Would you rather have an endless supply of chocolate, but never eat pizza again OR have an endless supply of pizza, but never eat chocolate again?

Laugh Point____/1

Add up your scores and record them below!

Player    /4
ROUND TOTAL

Player ♥2   /4
ROUND TOTAL

ROUND CHAMPION

Player

(DON'T FORGET TO EXPLAIN YOUR ANSWERS!)

Would you rather spend an entire day at school holding hands with your teacher, OR spend an entire recess sitting alone on top of your hands?

Laugh Point____/1

Would you rather have to eat a whole handful of sticky, melted gummy worms OR eat one chocolate-covered cricket?

Laugh Point____/1

Player

(DON'T FORGET TO EXPLAIN YOUR ANSWERS!)

Would you rather receive a bouquet of roses surrounded by a swarm of hungry bees, OR receive a teddy bear stuffed with rotten eggs?

Laugh Point____/1

Would you rather uncontrollably scream every time someone gave you a hug, OR get the hiccups for the entire day, every holiday?

Laugh Point____/1

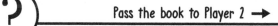

Player

(DON'T FORGET TO EXPLAIN YOUR ANSWERS!)

Would you rather your crush witness your squeaky shoes at the library OR witness you dropping all your books on the school bus steps?

Laugh Point____/1

Would you rather have a giant red lipstick kiss imprinted on your cheek for the rest of your life, OR have a nose that constantly glowed like Rudolph, the Red-Nosed Reindeer?

Laugh Point____/1

Player 2

(DON'T FORGET TO EXPLAIN YOUR ANSWERS!)

Would you rather slip on a puddle of jelly beans and fall flat on your face in front of your crush, OR accidentally spit on your crush's face when you were talking to them?

Laugh Point____/1

Would you rather celebrate Valentine's Day like Halloween, where everyone dressed in costumes OR like Easter, where everyone went hunting for their candy?

Laugh Point____/1

Time to score your points! →

Add up your scores and record them below!

Player  ____ /4
ROUND TOTAL

Player ❤2 ____ /4
ROUND TOTAL

ROUND CHAMPION

Player

(DON'T FORGET TO EXPLAIN YOUR ANSWERS!)

Would you rather miss a week of school and have all your classmates believe you had cooties, OR never get to miss a day of school all year, but also never get sick?

Laugh Point_____/1

Would you rather have to be in a kissing booth, but have bad breath OR be on a date with someone with stinky armpits?

Laugh Point_____/1

Player 1

(DON'T FORGET TO EXPLAIN YOUR ANSWERS!)

Would you rather only be able to say goodbye by giving someone a butterfly kiss with your eyelashes, OR have to hug every person that walked past you 10x?

Laugh Point____/1

Would you rather wear rings on your fingers made of worms OR wear a living snake as a necklace?

Laugh Point____/1

Pass the book to Player 2 →

Player 2

(DON'T FORGET TO EXPLAIN YOUR ANSWERS!)

Would you rather have a Love Goblin appear and make you do something embarrassing in front of your crush, OR have a Love Guru show up while you were talking to your crush, and made you tell them all of your feelings about them?

Laugh Point____/1

Would you rather your crush give you a lifetime supply of Hershey's kisses OR give you one kiss on the cheek?

Laugh Point____/1

Player 2

(DON'T FORGET TO EXPLAIN YOUR ANSWERS!)

Would you rather have heart-shaped sunglasses that could read everyone's minds to see their crush, OR have your own heartbeat be as loud as a drum whenever someone who had a crush on you was near?

Laugh Point____/1

Would you rather have your first name be "XOXO", OR say hello to everyone you saw only by yelling, "Smoochie smoothie!" and blowing them a kiss?

Laugh Point____/1

Time to score your points! →

Add up your scores and record them below!

Player  1   /4
ROUND TOTAL

Player 2   /4
ROUND TOTAL

ROUND CHAMPION

Add up all your points from each round.
The PLAYER with the most points is crowned
The Laugh Master!

In the event of a tie, continue to
Round 11 for the Tie-Breaker Round!

Player _____
GRAND TOTAL

Player  _____
GRAND TOTAL

ROUND 11

TIE-BREAKER
(WINNER TAKES ALL!)

Player 1

(DON'T FORGET TO EXPLAIN YOUR ANSWERS!)

Would you rather be in charge of writing the little messages on candy hearts, OR be in charge of licking and sealing EVERY single Valentine's card envelope?

Laugh Point____/1

Would you rather dress to impress, but end up staying home OR wear pajamas at your Valentine's school dance?

Laugh Point____/1

Player 1

(DON'T FORGET TO EXPLAIN YOUR ANSWERS!)

Would you rather have your wardrobe be made entirely out of sewn-together Tootsie Roll wrappers, OR have each of your teeth replaced by peanut M&Ms?

Laugh Point____/1

Would you rather spend your Valentine's Day in a forest hunting for Bigfoot, OR spend it swimming in a lake looking for the Loch Ness Monster?

Laugh Point____/1

Pass the book to Player 2 →

Player

(DON'T FORGET TO EXPLAIN YOUR ANSWERS!)

Would you rather eat a lollipop covered in dog fur OR a chocolate-covered worm?

Laugh Point____/1

Would you rather play a game of Truth or Dare with your friends, but you could only pick dare, OR spend your entire Valentine's Day under a spell that made you say whatever thought came into your mind, aloud?

Laugh Point____/1

Player

(DON'T FORGET TO EXPLAIN YOUR ANSWERS!)

Would you rather have all the stars in the sky turn into Starburst candies, OR have all of the bears in the forest turn into giant gummy bears?

Laugh Point____/1

Would you rather have your teacher read a love letter you wrote aloud to your entire class, OR have one of your classmates give you a smooch on the cheek in front of your school principal?

Laugh Point____/1

Time to score your points! →

Add up all your points from Round 11.
The PLAYER with the most points is crowned
The Laugh Master!

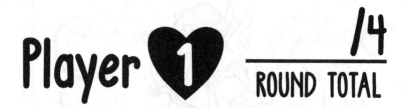

Player **1** _____ /4 ROUND TOTAL

Player **2** _____ /4 ROUND TOTAL

The Laugh Master

CHECK OUT OUR

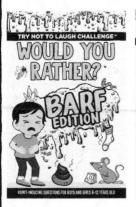

VISIT OUR AMAZON STORE AT:
WWW.AMAZON.COM/AUTHOR/CRAZYCOREY

OTHER JOKE BOOKS!

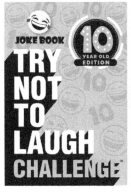
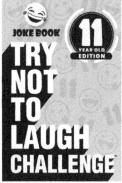

IF YOU HAVE ENJOYED OUR BOOK, WE WOULD LOVE FOR YOU TO REVIEW US ON AMAZON!

Made in the USA
Monee, IL
21 January 2021